HORN

101 HIT SONGS

Note: The keys in this book do not match the other wind instruments.

Available for
FLUTE, CLARINET, ALTO SAX, TENOR SAX, TRUMPET,
HORN, TROMBONE, VIOLIN, VIOLA, CELLO

ISBN 978-1-4950-7533-9

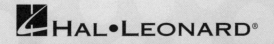

HAL•LEONARD®

7777 W. BLUEMOUND RD. P.O. BOX 13819 MILWAUKEE, WI 53213

Visit Hal Leonard Online at
www.halleonard.com

CONTENTS

4 All About That Bass

6 All of Me

5 Amazed

8 Apologize

10 Bad Day

12 Bad Romance

9 Beautiful

14 Beautiful Day

16 Beautiful in My Eyes

17 Because I Love You (The Postman Song)

18 Believe

20 Brave

22 Breakaway

24 Breathe

19 Butterfly Kisses

26 Call Me Maybe

28 Candle in the Wind 1997

29 Change the World

30 Chasing Cars

31 The Climb

32 Clocks

34 Countdown

36 Cruise

38 Cryin'

40 Die a Happy Man

42 Dilemma

33 Don't Know Why

44 Drift Away

46 Drops of Jupiter (Tell Me)

48 Fallin'

45 Fields of Gold

50 Firework

52 Foolish Games

54 Forever and for Always

56 Friends in Low Places

57 From a Distance

58 Genie in a Bottle

60 Get Lucky

62 Hello

64 Here and Now

66 Hero

68 Hey, Soul Sister

70 Ho Hey

72 Hold On, We're Going Home

74 Home

76 The House That Built Me

78 How Am I Supposed to Live Without You

61 How to Save a Life

80   I Finally Found Someone

82   I Gotta Feeling

84   I Kissed a Girl

86   I Swear

87   I Will Remember You

88   Jar of Hearts

90   Just the Way You Are

96   Let It Go

92   Lips of an Angel

94   Little Talks

98   Losing My Religion

100   Love Song

102   Love Story

104   More Than Words

97   Need You Now

106   No One

108   100 Years

110   The Power of Love

109   Rehab

112   Roar

113   Rolling in the Deep

114   Royals

115   Save the Best for Last

116   Say Something

118   Secrets

117   Shake It Off

120   She Will Be Loved

121   Smells Like Teen Spirit

122   Something to Talk About
(Let's Give Them Something to Talk About)

124   Stacy's Mom

126   Stay

123   Stay with Me

128   Stronger (What Doesn't Kill You)

130   Tears in Heaven

131   Teenage Dream

132   Thinking Out Loud

134   This Love

135   A Thousand Years

136   Till the World Ends

138   Uptown Funk

140   Viva La Vida

142   Waiting on the World to Change

144   We Belong Together

143   We Can't Stop

146   We Found Love

147   What Makes You Beautiful

148   When You Say Nothing at All

150   Yeah!

149   You Raise Me Up

152   You Were Meant for Me

154   You're Beautiful

155   You're Still the One

156   You've Got a Friend in Me

ALL ABOUT THAT BASS

Horn

Words and Music by KEVIN KADISH
and MEGHAN TRAINOR

AMAZED

Horn

Words and Music by MARV GREEN,
CHRIS LINDSEY and AIMEE MAYO

Moderately slow

ALL OF ME

HORN

Words and Music by JOHN STEPHENS
and TOBY GAD

Slowly, in 2

1st time D.C.
2nd Time Fine

D.S. al Fine
(take 1st ending)

APOLOGIZE

HORN

Words and Music by
RYAN TEDDER

BEAUTIFUL

Horn

Words and Music by
LINDA PERRY

BAD DAY

HORN

Words and Music by
DANIEL POWTER

Moderate groove

D.S. al Coda

CODA

BAD ROMANCE

HORN

Words and Music by STEFANI GERMANOTTA
and NADIR KHAYAT

BEAUTIFUL DAY

Horn

Words by BONO
Music by U2

BEAUTIFUL IN MY EYES

HORN

Words and Music by
JOSHUA KADISON

BECAUSE I LOVE YOU
(The Postman Song)

HORN

Words and Music by
WARREN BROOKS

BELIEVE

Horn

Words and Music by BRIAN HIGGINS,
STUART McLENNEN, PAUL BARRY,
STEPHEN TORCH, MATT GRAY
and TIM POWELL

BUTTERFLY KISSES

Horn

Words and Music by BOB CARLISLE
and RANDY THOMAS

BRAVE

HORN

Words and Music by SARA BAREILLES
and JACK ANTONOFF

Moderately

BREAKAWAY

from THE PRINCESS DIARIES 2: ROYAL ENGAGEMENT

Horn

Words and Music by BRIDGET BENENATE,
AVRIL LAVIGNE and MATTHEW GERRARD

BREATHE

HORN

Words and Music by HOLLY LAMAR
and STEPHANIE BENTLEY

CALL ME MAYBE

Horn

Words and Music by CARLY RAE JEPSEN,
JOSHUA RAMSAY and TAVISH CROWE

To Coda

D.S. al Coda
(no repeat)

CODA

CANDLE IN THE WIND 1997

HORN

Words and Music by ELTON JOHN
and BERNIE TAUPIN

Slowly, in 2

CHANGE THE WORLD

featured on the Motion Picture Soundtrack PHENOMENON

Horn

Words and Music by WAYNE KIRKPATRICK,
GORDON KENNEDY and TOMMY SIMS

Moderately

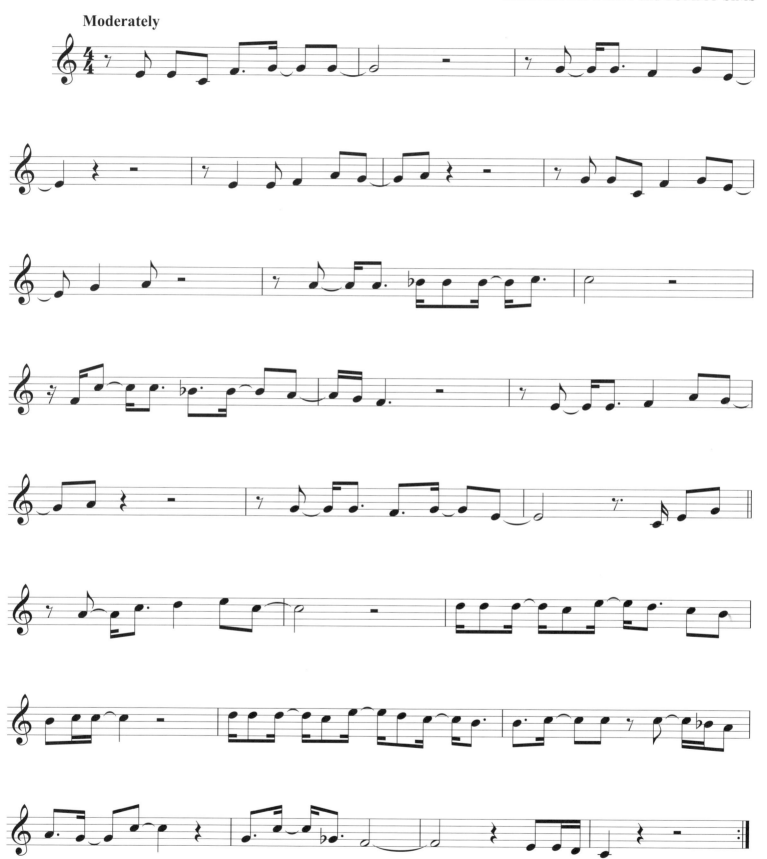

CHASING CARS

Horn

Words and Music by GARY LIGHTBODY,
TOM SIMPSON, PAUL WILSON,
JONATHAN QUINN and NATHAN CONNOLLY

THE CLIMB
from HANNAH MONTANA: THE MOVIE

HORN

Words and Music by JESSI ALEXANDER
and JON MABE

CLOCKS

HORN

Words and Music by GUY BERRYMAN,
JON BUCKLAND, WILL CHAMPION
and CHRIS MARTIN

DON'T KNOW WHY

HORN

Words and Music by
JESSE HARRIS

COUNTDOWN

Horn

Words and Music by BEYONCÉ KNOWLES,
CAINON LAMB, JULIE FROST, MICHAEL BIVINS,
ESTHER DEAN, TERIUS NASH, SHEA TAYLOR,
NATHAN MORRIS and WANYA MORRIS

2nd time, D.C. al Coda

CODA

CRUISE

Horn

Words and Music by CHASE RICE,
TYLER HUBBARD, BRIAN KELLEY,
JOEY MOI and JESSE RICE

CRYIN'

Horn

Words and Music by STEVEN TYLER,
JOE PERRY and TAYLOR RHODES

Moderately slow, in 2

DIE A HAPPY MAN

Horn

Words and Music by THOMAS RHETT,
JOE SPARGUR and SEAN DOUGLAS

Moderately slow

DILEMMA

HORN

Words and Music by CORNELL HAYNES,
ANTWON MAKER, KENNETH GAMBLE
and BUNNY SIGLER

Fine

2nd time, D.S. al Fine

DRIFT AWAY

HORN

Words and Music by
MENTOR WILLIAMS

FIELDS OF GOLD

HORN

Music and Lyrics by
STING

DROPS OF JUPITER
(Tell Me)

Horn

Words and Music by PAT MONAHAN,
JAMES STAFFORD, ROBERT HOTCHKISS,
CHARLES COLIN and SCOTT UNDERWOOD

47

D.S. al Coda

CODA

FALLIN'

Horn

Words and Music by
ALICIA KEYS

49

FIREWORK

Horn

Words and Music by KATY PERRY,
MIKKEL ERIKSEN, TOR ERIK HERMANSEN,
ESTHER DEAN and SANDY WILHELM

Moderately

51

FOOLISH GAMES

HORN

Words and Music by
JEWEL KILCHER

Slowly

FOREVER AND FOR ALWAYS

Horn

Words and Music by SHANIA TWAIN
and R.J. LANGE

Moderately, in 2

FRIENDS IN LOW PLACES

HORN

Words and Music by DeWAYNE BLACKWELL
and EARL BUD LEE

Moderately

FROM A DISTANCE

HORN

Words and Music by
JULIE GOLD

GENIE IN A BOTTLE

Horn

Words and Music by STEVE KIPNER,
DAVID FRANK and PAMELA SHEYNE

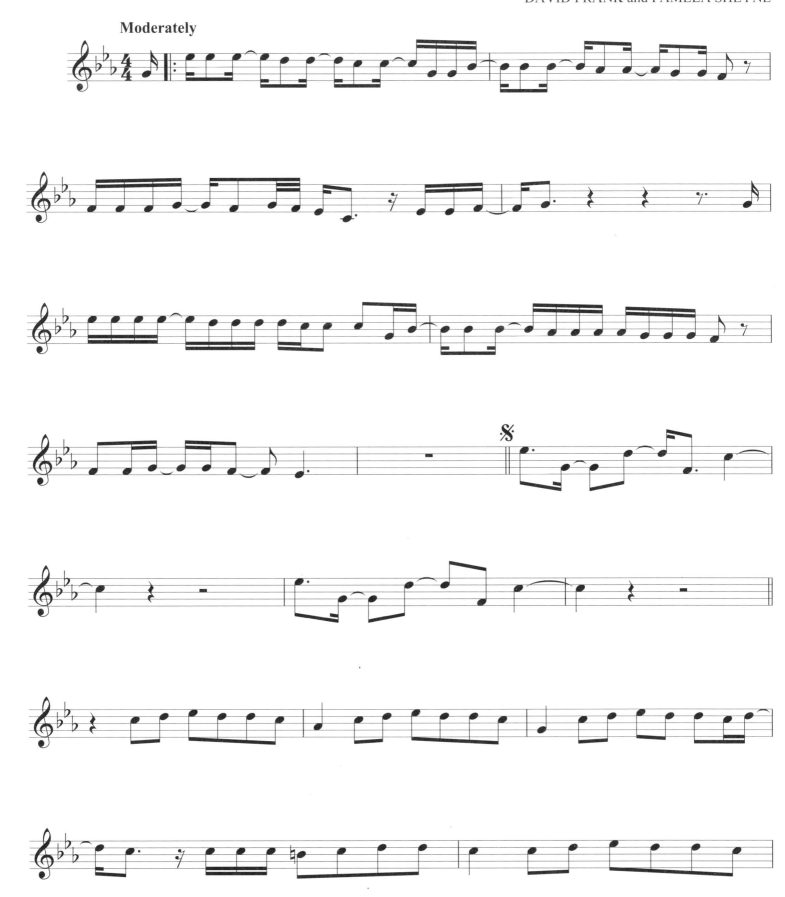

GET LUCKY

Horn

Words and Music by THOMAS BANGALTER,
GUY MANUEL HOMEM CHRISTO, NILE RODGERS
and PHARRELL WILLIAMS

HOW TO SAVE A LIFE

HORN

Words and Music by JOSEPH KING
and ISAAC SLADE

HELLO

Horn

Words and Music by ADELE ADKINS
and GREG KURSTIN

HERE AND NOW

Horn

Words and Music by TERRY STEELE
and DAVID ELLIOT

Moderately slow

HERO

HORN

Words and Music by ENRIQUE IGLESIAS,
PAUL BARRY and MARK TAYLOR

Moderately slow

HEY, SOUL SISTER

Horn

Words and Music by PAT MONAHAN,
ESPEN LIND and AMUND BJORKLUND

HO HEY

HORN

Words and Music by JEREMY FRAITES
and WESLEY SCHULTZ

Moderately slow, in 2

HOLD ON, WE'RE GOING HOME

Horn

Words and Music by AUBREY GRAHAM,
PAUL JEFFERIES, NOAH SHEBIB,
JORDAN ULLMAN and MAJID AL-MASKATI

HOME

HORN

Words and Music by GREG HOLDEN
and DREW PEARSON

Moderately, in 2

THE HOUSE THAT BUILT ME

Horn

Words and Music by TOM DOUGLAS
and ALLEN SHAMBLIN

77

HOW AM I SUPPOSED TO LIVE WITHOUT YOU

Horn

Words and Music by MICHAEL BOLTON
and DOUG JAMES

I FINALLY FOUND SOMEONE

from THE MIRROR HAS TWO FACES

Horn

Words and Music by BARBRA STREISAND,
MARVIN HAMLISCH, R.J. LANGE
and BRYAN ADAMS

I GOTTA FEELING

Horn

Words and Music by WILL ADAMS,
ALLAN PINEDA, JAIME GOMEZ, STACY FERGUSON,
DAVID GUETTA and FREDERIC RIESTERER

Moderately fast

I KISSED A GIRL

Horn

Words and Music by KATY PERRY,
CATHY DENNIS, MAX MARTIN
and LUKASZ GOTTWALD

I SWEAR

HORN

Words and Music by FRANK MYERS
and GARY BAKER

Moderately

I WILL REMEMBER YOU
Theme from THE BROTHERS McMULLEN

Horn

Words and Music by SARAH McLACHLAN,
SEAMUS EGAN and DAVE MERENDA

JAR OF HEARTS

Horn

Words and Music by BARRETT YERETSIAN,
CHRISTINA PERRI and DREW LAWRENCE

JUST THE WAY YOU ARE

HORN

Words and Music by BRUNO MARS,
ARI LEVINE, PHILIP LAWRENCE,
KHARI CAIN and KHALIL WALTON

Moderately

91

LIPS OF AN ANGEL

Words and Music by AUSTIN WINKLER,
ROSS HANSON, LLOYD GARVEY, MARK KING,
MICHAEL RODDEN and BRIAN HOWES

Horn

LITTLE TALKS

Horn

Words and Music by
OF MONSTERS AND MEN

LET IT GO

HORN

Words and Music by JAMES BAY
and PAUL BARRY

NEED YOU NOW

HORN

Words and Music by HILLARY SCOTT,
CHARLES KELLEY, DAVE HAYWOOD
and JOSH KEAR

LOSING MY RELIGION

HORN

Words and Music by WILLIAM BERRY,
PETER BUCK, MICHAEL MILLS
and MICHAEL STIPE

LOVE SONG

Horn

Words and Music by
SARA BAREILLES

LOVE STORY

HORN

Words and Music by
TAYLOR SWIFT

Moderately

MORE THAN WORDS

HORN

Words and Music by NUNO BETTENCOURT
and GARY CHERONE

Moderately slow

NO ONE

Words and Music by ALICIA KEYS,
KERRY BROTHERS, JR. and GEORGE HARRY

HORN

To Coda

D.S. al Coda

CODA

100 YEARS

HORN

Words and Music by
JOHN ONDRASIK

REHAB

HORN

Words and Music by
AMY WINEHOUSE

THE POWER OF LOVE

Horn

Words by MARY SUSAN APPLEGATE
and JENNIFER RUSH
Music by CANDY DEROUGE
and GUNTHER MENDE

Slowly

ROAR

HORN

Words and Music by KATY PERRY,
LUKASZ GOTTWALD, MAX MARTIN,
BONNIE McKEE and HENRY WALTER

ROLLING IN THE DEEP

HORN

Words and Music by ADELE ADKINS
and PAUL EPWORTH

ROYALS

HORN

Words and Music by ELLA YELICH-O'CONNOR
and JOEL LITTLE

SAVE THE BEST FOR LAST

Horn

Words and Music by WENDY WALDMAN,
PHIL GALDSTON and JON LIND

SAY SOMETHING

Horn

Words and Music by IAN AXEL,
CHAD VACCARINO and MIKE CAMPBELL

Very slowly, in 4

SHAKE IT OFF

Horn

Words and Music by TAYLOR SWIFT,
MAX MARTIN and SHELLBACK

SECRETS

HORN

Words and Music by
RYAN TEDDER

Moderately slow, in 2

SHE WILL BE LOVED

HORN

Words and Music by ADAM LEVINE
and JAMES VALENTINE

SMELLS LIKE TEEN SPIRIT

HORN

Words and Music by KURT COBAIN,
KRIST NOVOSELIC and DAVE GROHL

SOMETHING TO TALK ABOUT

(Let's Give Them Something to Talk About)

HORN

Words and Music by
SHIRLEY EIKHARD

STAY WITH ME

HORN

Words and Music by SAM SMITH,
JAMES NAPIER, WILLIAM EDWARD PHILLIPS,
TOM PETTY and JEFF LYNNE

STACY'S MOM

HORN

Words and Music by CHRIS COLLINGWOOD
and ADAM SCHLESINGER

STAY

HORN

Words and Music by MIKKY EKKO
and JUSTIN PARKER

Moderately

STRONGER
(What Doesn't Kill You)

Horn

Words and Music by GREG KURSTIN,
JORGEN ELOFSSON, DAVID GAMSON
and ALEXANDRA TAMPOSI

2nd time, to Coda

3rd time, Fine

D.S. al Coda

CODA

D.S. al Fine

TEARS IN HEAVEN

Horn

Words and Music by ERIC CLAPTON
and WILL JENNINGS

TEENAGE DREAM

HORN

Words and Music by KATY PERRY,
BONNIE McKEE, LUKASZ GOTTWALD,
MAX MARTIN and BENJAMIN LEVIN

THINKING OUT LOUD

Horn

Words and Music by ED SHEERAN
and AMY WADGE

THIS LOVE

HORN

Words and Music by ADAM LEVINE
and JESSE CARMICHAEL

Moderate Rock

A THOUSAND YEARS

from the Summit Entertainment film THE TWILIGHT SAGE: BREAKING DAWN - Part 1

Horn

Words and Music by DAVID HODGES
and CHRISTINA PERRI

TILL THE WORLD ENDS

HORN

Words and Music by LUKASZ GOTTWALD,
MAX MARTIN, KESHA SEBERT
and ALEXANDER KRONLUND

Moderately fast

UPTOWN FUNK

HORN

Words and Music by MARK RONSON,
BRUNO MARS, PHILIP LAWRENCE, JEFF BHASKER, DEVON GALLASPY,
NICHOLAUS WILLIAMS, LONNIE SIMMONS, RONNIE WILSON,
CHARLES WILSON, RUDOLPH TAYLOR and ROBERT WILSON

VIVA LA VIDA

Words and Music by GUY BERRYMAN,
JON BUCKLAND, WILL CHAMPION
and CHRIS MARTIN

HORN

Moderately

WAITING ON THE WORLD TO CHANGE

HORN

Words and Music by
JOHN MAYER

WE CAN'T STOP

Horn

Words and Music by MILEY CYRUS,
THERON THOMAS, TIMOTHY THOMAS, MICHAEL WILLIAMS,
PIERRE SLAUGHTER, DOUGLAS DAVIS and RICKY WALTERS

Moderately slow

WE BELONG TOGETHER

Horn

Words and Music by MARIAH CAREY,
JERMAINE DUPRI, MANUEL SEAL, JOHNTA AUSTIN,
DARNELL BRISTOL, KENNETH EDMONDS, SIDNEY JOHNSON,
PATRICK MOTEN, BOBBY WOMACK and SANDRA SULLY

Slow Soul

WE FOUND LOVE

Horn

Words and Music by
CALVIN HARRIS

WHAT MAKES YOU BEAUTIFUL

HORN

Words and Music by SAVAN KOTECHA,
RAMI YACOUB and CARL FALK

WHEN YOU SAY NOTHING AT ALL

Horn

Words and Music by DON SCHLITZ
and PAUL OVERSTREET

YOU RAISE ME UP

HORN

Words and Music by BRENDAN GRAHAM
and ROLF LOVLAND

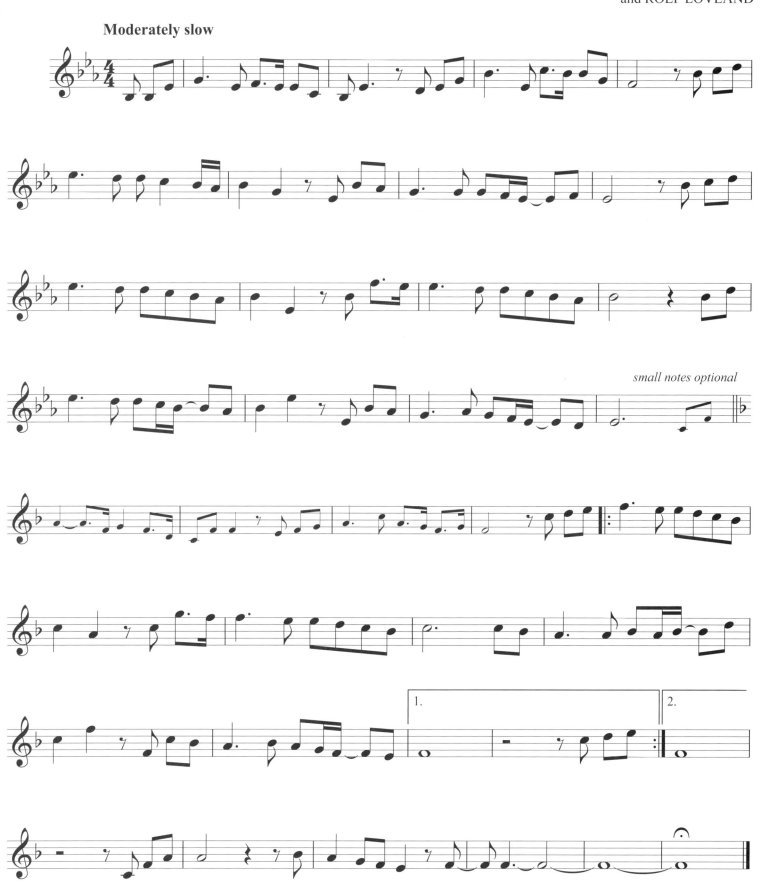

YEAH!

Horn

Words and Music by JAMES PHILLIPS,
LA MARQUIS JEFFERSON, CHRISTOPHER BRIDGES,
JONATHAN SMITH and SEAN GARRETT

YOU WERE MEANT FOR ME

Horn

Words and Music by JEWEL MURRAY
and STEVE POLTZ

YOU'RE BEAUTIFUL

Words and Music by JAMES BLUNT,
SACHA SKARBEK and AMANDA GHOST

Horn

YOU'RE STILL THE ONE

Horn

Words and Music by SHANIA TWAIN
and R.J. LANGE

YOU'VE GOT A FRIEND IN ME

from Walt Disney's TOY STORY

HORN

Music and Lyrics by
RANDY NEWMAN

101 SONGS

BIG COLLECTIONS OF FAVORITE SONGS ARRANGED FOR SOLO INSTRUMENTALISTS.

101 BROADWAY SONGS

00154199 Flute.............$15.99
00154200 Clarinet.......$15.99
00154201 Alto Sax.......$15.99
00154202 Tenor Sax....$16.99
00154203 Trumpet.......$15.99
00154204 Horn.............$15.99
00154205 Trombone...$15.99
00154206 Violin.............$15.99
0154207 Viola.............................$15.99
0154208 Cello.............................$15.99

101 DISNEY SONGS

00244104 Flute.............$17.99
00244106 Clarinet.......$17.99
00244107 Alto Sax.......$17.99
00244108 Tenor Sax...$17.99
00244109 Trumpet.......$17.99
00244112 Horn.............$17.99
00244120 Trombone...$17.99
00244121 Violin.............$17.99
00244125 Viola.............................$17.99
00244126 Cello.............................$17.99

101 MOVIE HITS

00158087 Flute.............$15.99
00158088 Clarinet.......$15.99
00158089 Alto Sax......$15.99
00158090 Tenor Sax...$15.99
00158091 Trumpet.......$15.99
00158092 Horn.............$15.99
00158093 Trombone...$15.99
00158094 Violin.............$15.99
00158095 Viola.............................$15.99
00158096 Cello.............................$15.99

101 CHRISTMAS SONGS

00278637 Flute.............$15.99
00278638 Clarinet.......$15.99
00278639 Alto Sax......$15.99
00278640 Tenor Sax..$15.99
00278641 Trumpet........$15.99
00278642 Horn.............$14.99
00278643 Trombone...$15.99
00278644 Violin.............$15.99
0278645 Viola.............................$15.99
0278646 Cello.............................$15.99

101 HIT SONGS

00194561 Flute.............$17.99
00197182 Clarinet.........$17.99
00197183 Alto Sax........$17.99
00197184 Tenor Sax.....$17.99
00197185 Trumpet.........$17.99
00197186 Horn.............$17.99
00197187 Trombone.....$17.99
00197188 Violin.............$17.99
00197189 Viola.............................$17.99
00197190 Cello.............................$17.99

101 POPULAR SONGS

00224722 Flute.............$17.99
00224723 Clarinet.......$17.99
00224724 Alto Sax......$17.99
00224725 Tenor Sax...$17.99
00224726 Trumpet.......$17.99
00224727 Horn.............$17.99
00224728 Trombone...$17.99
00224729 Violin.............$17.99
00224730 Viola.............................$17.99
00224731 Cello.............................$17.99

101 CLASSICAL THEMES

00155315 Flute.............$15.99
00155317 Clarinet.........$15.99
00155318 Alto Sax.......$15.99
00155319 Tenor Sax.....$15.99
00155320 Trumpet......$15.99
00155321 Horn.............$15.99
00155322 Trombone...$15.99
00155323 Violin.............$15.99
0155324 Viola.............................$15.99
0155325 Cello.............................$15.99

101 JAZZ SONGS

00146363 Flute..............$15.99
00146364 Clarinet.........$15.99
00146366 Alto Sax.......$15.99
00146367 Tenor Sax....$15.99
00146368 Trumpet........$15.99
00146369 Horn.............$14.99
00146370 Trombone...$15.99
00146371 Violin.............$15.99
00146372 Viola.............................$15.99
00146373 Cello.............................$15.99

101 MOST BEAUTIFUL SONGS

00291023 Flute.............$16.99
00291041 Clarinet.........$16.99
00291042 Alto Sax........$17.99
00291043 Tenor Sax.....$17.99
00291044 Trumpet.......$16.99
00291045 Horn.............$16.99
00291046 Trombone...$16.99
00291047 Violin.............$16.99
00291048 Viola.............................$16.99
00291049 Cello.............................$17.99

See complete song lists and sample pages at www.halleonard.com

HAL•LEONARD®
www.halleonard.com

Prices, contents and availability subject to change without notice.

101 TIPS FROM HAL LEONARD

STUFF ALL THE PROS KNOW AND USE

Ready to take your skills to the next level? These books present valuable how-to insight that musicians of all styles and levels can benefit from. The text, photos, music, diagrams and accompanying audio provide a terrific, easy-to-use resource for a variety of topics.

101 HAMMOND B-3 TIPS
by Brian Charette
Topics include: funky scales and modes; unconventional harmonies; creative chord voicings; cool drawbar settings; ear-grabbing special effects; professional gigging advice; practicing effectively; making good use of the pedals; and much more!
00128918 Book/Online Audio $14.99

101 HARMONICA TIPS
by Steve Cohen
Topics include: techniques, position playing, soloing, accompaniment, the blues, equipment, performance, maintenance, and much more!
00821040 Book/Online Audio $17.99

101 CELLO TIPS—2ND EDITION
by Angela Schmidt
Topics include: bowing techniques, non-classical playing, electric cellos, accessories, gig tips, practicing, recording and much more!
00149094 Book/Online Audio $14.99

101 FLUTE TIPS
by Elaine Schmidt
Topics include: selecting the right flute for you, finding the right teacher, warm-up exercises, practicing effectively, taking good care of your flute, gigging advice, staying and playing healthy, and much more.
00119883 Book/CD Pack..................................$14.99

101 SAXOPHONE TIPS
by Eric Morones
Topics include: techniques; maintenance; equipment; practicing; recording; performance; and much more!
00311082 Book/CD Pack..................................$19.99

101 TRUMPET TIPS
by Scott Barnard
Topics include: techniques, articulation, tone production, soloing, exercises, special effects, equipment, performance, maintenance and much more.
00312082 Book/CD Pack..................................$14.99

101 UPRIGHT BASS TIPS
by Andy McKee
Topics include: right- and left-hand technique, improvising and soloing, practicing, proper care of the instrument, ear training, performance, and much more.
00102009 Book/Online Audio $14.99

101 BASS TIPS
by Gary Willis
Topics include: techniques, improvising and soloing, equipment, practicing, ear training, performance, theory, and much more.
00695542 Book/Online Audio $19.99

101 DRUM TIPS—2ND EDITION
Topics include: grooves, practicing, warming up, tuning, gear, performance, and much more!
00151936 Book/Online Audio $14.99

101 FIVE-STRING BANJO TIPS
by Fred Sokolow
Topics include: techniques, ear training, performance, and much more!
00696647 Book/CD Pack..................................$14.99

101 GUITAR TIPS
by Adam St. James
Topics include: scales, music theory, truss rod adjustments, proper recording studio set-ups, and much more. The book also features snippets of advice from some of the most celebrated guitarists and producers in the music business.
00695737 Book/Online Audio $17.99

101 MANDOLIN TIPS
by Fred Sokolow
Topics include: playing tips, practicing tips, accessories, mandolin history and lore, practical music theory, and much more!
00119493 Book/Online Audio $14.99

101 RECORDING TIPS
by Adam St. James
This book contains recording tips, suggestions, and advice learned firsthand from legendary producers, engineers, and artists. These tricks of the trade will improve anyone's home or pro studio recordings.
00311035 Book/CD Pack..................................$14.95

101 UKULELE TIPS
by Fred Sokolow with Ronny Schiff
Topics include: techniques, improvising and soloing, equipment, practicing, ear training, performance, uke history and lore, and much more!
00696596 Book/Online Audio $15.99

101 VIOLIN TIPS
by Angela Schmidt
Topics include: bowing techniques, non-classical playing, electric violins, accessories, gig tips, practicing, recording, and much more!
00842672 Book/CD Pack..................................$14.99

Prices, contents and availability subject to change without notice.

HAL•LEONARD®
www.halleonard.com

ANewTuneADay™

 Music Sales America

Since it first appeared in the 1930s, the concise, clear content of the best-selling A Tune a Day series has revolutionized music-making in the classroom and the home. Now, for the first time, C. Paul Herfurth's original books have been completely rewritten on clear, uncluttered pages with new music and the latest in instrument technique for a new generation of musicians.

A New Tune a Day books have the same logical, gentle pace, and keen attention to detail, but with a host of innovations: the inclusion of an audio CD – with actual performances and backing tracks – will make practice even more fun and exciting, and the explanatory diagrams and photographs will help the student to achieve the perfect technique and tone. Useful pull-out fingering charts are also included.

The **DVDs** show you the basics from how to set up your instrument to playing your first notes. They take you through the first few pages of the book ensuring you get off to a good start. Authored for Zone 0, these DVDs also provide excellent advice and tips from a professional player.

Each **Book 1** contains:
• advice on audio equipment
• instructions for effective technique and comfortable posture
• explanatory section on reading music
• great music including duets and rounds
• tests to check progress and comprehension

Each **Book 2** contains:
• tips for technique
• improvising hints
• great music including duets and ensemble pieces

The **Performance Pieces** books are inspiring collections of favorite melodies, clearly presented with a play-along CD for the advanced beginner. These pieces have been chosen and arranged to build a repertoire for performance and for fun, and include well-known classical melodies, showstoppers, jazz hits, folk songs, popular tunes, and film & TV themes. These books include chord symbols for accompaniment on piano, keyboard or guitar.

A NEW TUNE A DAY – ACOUSTIC GUITAR
by John Blackwell
Book 1
_____ 14022730 Book/CD Pack...........................$9.99

A NEW TUNE A DAY – ALTO SAXOPHONE
by Ned Bennett
Book 1
_____ 14022731 Book/CD/DVD Pack $17.99
_____ 14022747 Book/CD Pack...........................$14.99
Book 2
_____ 14022732 Book/CD Pack...........................$9.95
Performance Pieces
_____ 14022755 Book/CD Pack...........................$12.95

A NEW TUNE A DAY – CELLO
by Janet Coles
Book 1
_____ 14022737 Book/CD/DVD Pack $17.99
Performance Pieces
_____ 14022756 Book/CD Pack...........................$12.95

A NEW TUNE A DAY – CLARINET
by Ned Bennett
Book 1
_____ 14022738 Book/CD/DVD Pack $17.95
_____ 14022749 Book/CD Pack...........................$12.99
Book 2
_____ 14022739 Book/CD Pack...........................$9.95
Performance Pieces
_____ 14022757 Book/CD Pack...........................$12.95

A NEW TUNE A DAY – DRUMS
by Chris Baker
Book 1
_____ 14022750 Book/CD Pack...........................$9.95

A NEW TUNE A DAY – ELECTRIC GUITAR
by Pete Kershaw
Book 1
_____ 14022743 Book/CD Pack...........................$9.95

A NEW TUNE A DAY – FLUTE
by Ned Bennett
Book 2
_____ 14022745 Book/CD Pack...........................$9.95
Performance Pieces for Flute
_____ 14022758 Book/CD Pack...........................$12.95

A NEW TUNE A DAY – PIANO
by Moira Hayward
Book 1
_____ 14022762 Book/CD/DVD Pack $17.95
_____ 14022763 Book/CD Pack...........................$9.99

A NEW TUNE A DAY – TENOR SAXOPHONE
by John Blackwell
Book 1
_____ 14022764 Book/CD/DVD Pack $17.9
_____ 14022765 Book/CD Pack...........................$9.95

A NEW TUNE A DAY – TROMBONE
by Amos Miller
Book 1
_____ 14022766 Book/CD/DVD Pack $17.95
Performance Pieces
_____ 14022759 Book/CD Pack...........................$12.95

A NEW TUNE A DAY – TRUMPET
by Brian Thomson
Book 1
_____ 14022767 Book/CD/DVD Pack $17.95
Performance Pieces
_____ 14022760 Book/CD Pack...........................$12.95

A NEW TUNE A DAY – VIOLA
by Sarah Pope
Book 1
_____ 14022768 Book/CD/DVD Pack $17.95
_____ 14022769 Book/CD Pack...........................$9.95
_____ 14037519 Book Only...............................$6.50

A NEW TUNE A DAY – VIOLIN
by Sarah Pope
Book 1
_____ 14022770 Book/CD/DVD Pack $17.99
Performance Pieces
_____ 14022761 Book/CD Pack...........................$12.99

HAL•LEONARD®

Prices, contents and availability subject to change without notice.

www.halleonard.com

THE ULTIMATE COLLECTION OF
FAKE BOOKS

The Real Book – Sixth Edition

Hal Leonard proudly presents the first legitimate and legal editions of these books ever produced. These bestselling titles are mandatory for anyone who plays jazz! Over 400 songs, including: All By Myself • Dream a Little Dream of Me • God Bless the Child • Like Someone in Love • When I Fall in Love • and more.

00240221 Volume 1, C Instruments......................$45.00
00240224 Volume 1, B♭ Instruments.....................$45.00
00240225 Volume 1, E♭ Instruments.....................$45.00
00240226 Volume 1, BC Instruments.....................$45.00

Go to halleonard.com
to view all *Real Books* available

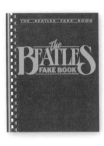

The Beatles Fake Book

200 of the Beatles' hits: All You Need Is Love • Blackbird • Can't Buy Me Love • Day Tripper • Eleanor Rigby • The Fool on the Hill • Hey Jude • In My Life • Let It Be • Michelle • Norwegian Wood (This Bird Has Flown) • Penny Lane • Revolution • She Loves You • Twist and Shout • With a Little Help from My Friends • Yesterday • and many more!
00240069 C Instruments...........$39.99

The Best Fake Book Ever

More than 1,000 songs from all styles of music: All My Loving • At the Hop • Cabaret • Dust in the Wind • Fever • Hello, Dolly • Hey Jude • King of the Road • Longer • Misty • Route 66 • Sentimental Journey • Somebody • Song Sung Blue • Spinning Wheel • Unchained Melody • We Will Rock You • What a Wonderful World • Wooly Bully • Y.M.C.A. • and more.

00290239 C Instruments.....................................$49.99
00240084 E♭ Instruments....................................$49.95

The Celtic Fake Book

Over 400 songs from Ireland, Scotland and Wales: Auld Lang Syne • Barbara Allen • Danny Boy • Finnegan's Wake • The Galway Piper • Irish Rover • Loch Lomond • Molly Malone • My Bonnie Lies Over the Ocean • My Wild Irish Rose • That's an Irish Lullaby • and more. Includes Gaelic lyrics where applicable and a pronunciation guide.
00240153 C Instruments...........$25.00

Classic Rock Fake Book

Over 250 of the best rock songs of all time: American Woman • Beast of Burden • Carry On Wayward Son • Dream On • Free Ride • Hurts So Good • I Shot the Sheriff • Layla • My Generation • Nights in White Satin • Owner of a Lonely Heart • Rhiannon • Roxanne • Summer of '69 • We Will Rock You • You Ain't Seen Nothin' Yet • and lots more!

00240108 C Instruments...................................$35.00

Classical Fake Book

This unprecedented, amazingly comprehensive reference includes over 850 classical themes and melodies for all classical music lovers. Includes everything from Renaissance music to Vivaldi and Mozart to Mendelssohn. Lyrics in the original language are included when appropriate.
00240044...$39.99

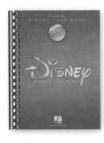

The Disney Fake Book

Even more Disney favorites, including: The Bare Necessities • Can You Feel the Love Tonight • Circle of Life • How Do You Know? • Let It Go • Part of Your World • Reflection • Some Day My Prince Will Come • When I See an Elephant Fly • You'll Be in My Heart • and many more.

00175311 C Instruments...........$34.99
Disney characters & artwork TM & © 2021 Disney

The Folksong Fake Book

Over 1,000 folksongs: Bury Me Not on the Lone Prairie • Clementine • The Erie Canal • Go, Tell It on the Mountain • Home on the Range • Kumbaya • Michael Row the Boat Ashore • Shenandoah • Simple Gifts • Swing Low, Sweet Chariot • When Johnny Comes Marching Home • Yankee Doodle • and many more.
00240151 ....$34.99

The Hal Leonard Real Jazz Standards Fake Book

Over 250 standards in easy-to-read authentic hand-written jazz engravings: Ain't Misbehavin' • Blue Skies • Crazy He Calls Me • Desafinado (Off Key) • Fever • How High the Moon • It Don't Mean a Thing (If It Ain't Got That Swing) • Lazy River • Mood Indigo • Old Devil Moon • Route 66 • Satin Doll • Witchcraft • and more.

00240161 C Instruments..............................$45.00

The Hymn Fake Book

Nearly 1,000 multi-denominational hymns perfect for church musicians or hobbyists: Amazing Grace • Christ the Lord Is Risen Today • For the Beauty of the Earth • It Is Well with My Soul • A Mighty Fortress Is Our God • O for a Thousand Tongues to Sing • Praise to the Lord, the Almighty • Take My Life and Let It Be • What a Friend We Have in Jesus • and hundreds more!

00240145 C Instruments..............................$29.99

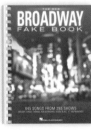

The New Broadway Fake Book

This amazing collection includes 645 songs from 285 shows: All I Ask of You • Any Dream Will Do • Close Every Door • Consider Yourself • Dancing Queen • Mack the Knife • Mamma Mia • Memory • The Phantom of the Opera • Popular • Strike up the Band • and more!

00138905 C Instruments...........$45.00

The Praise & Worship Fake Book

Over 400 songs including: Amazing Grace (My Chains Are Gone) • Cornerstone • Everlasting God • Great Are You Lord • In Christ Alone • Mighty to Save • Open the Eyes of My Heart • Shine, Jesus, Shine • This Is Amazing Grace • and more.

00160838 C Instruments...........$39.99
00240324 B♭ Instruments.........$34.99

Three Chord Songs Fake Book

200 classic and contemporary 3-chord tunes in melody/lyric/chord format: Ain't No Sunshine • Bang a Gong (Get It On) • Cold, Cold Heart • Don't Worry, Be Happy • Give Me One Reason • I Got You (I Feel Good) • Kiss • Me and Bobby McGee • Rock This Town • Werewolves of London • You Don't Mess Around with Jim • and more.

00240387...$34.99

The Ultimate Christmas Fake Book

The 6th edition of this bestseller features over 270 traditional and contemporary Christmas hits: Have Yourself a Merry Little Christmas • I'll Be Home for Christmas O Come, All Ye Faithful (Adeste Fideles) • Santa Baby • Winter Wonderland • and more.
00147215 C Instruments...........$30.00

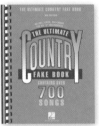

The Ultimate Country Fake Book

This book includes over 700 of your favorite country hits: Always on My Mind • Boot Scootin' Boogie • Crazy • Down at the Twist and Shout • Forever and Ever, Amen • Friends in Low Places • The Gambler • Jambalaya • King of the Road • Sixteen Tons • There's a Tear in My Beer • Your Cheatin' Heart • and hundreds more.

00240049 C Instruments....................................$49.99

The Ultimate Fake Book

Includes over 1,200 hits: Blue Skies • Body and Soul • Endless Love • Isn't It Romantic? • Memory • Mona Lisa • Moon River • Operator • Piano Man • Roxanne • Satin Doll • Shout • Small World • Smile • Speak Softly, Love • Strawberry Fields Forever • Tears in Heaven • Unforgettable • hundreds more!

00240024 C Instruments...........$55.00
00240026 B♭ Instruments.....................$49.95

The Ultimate Jazz Fake Book

This must-own collection includes 635 songs spanning all jazz styles from more than 9 decades. Songs include: Maple Leaf Rag • Basin Street Blues • A Night in Tunisia • Lullaby of Birdland • The Girl from Ipanema • Bag's Groove • I Can't Get Started • All the Things You Are • and many more!

00240079 C Instruments................$45.00
00240080 B♭ Instruments...............$45.00
00240081 E♭ Instruments...............$45.00

The Ultimate Rock Pop Fake Book

This amazing collection features nearly 550 rock and pop hits: American Pie • Bohemian Rhapsody • Born to Be Wild • Clocks • Dancing with Myself • Eye of the Tiger • Proud Mary • Rocket Man • Should I Stay or Should I Go • Total Eclipse of the Heart • Unchained Melody • When Doves Cry • Y.M.C.A. • You Raise Me Up • and more.

00240310 C Instruments......................................$39.99